And there is, for me, no difference between writing a good poem and moving into sunlight against the body of a woman I love.

-Audre Lorde, Sister Outsider: Essays and Speeches

LOVE POEMS

Tammy James

Love Poems Copyright © 2017 by Tammy James

ISBN: 978-0-9998693-0-7

First Edition: December 2017
Publication Date: January 2018

10 9 8 7 6 5 4 3 2 1

to the women who are not afraid to love loudly

there are rich undertones of galaxies beneath her flesh. i wish she could see the way the light pours from her. even her darkness is astounding. i have memorized the sound love makes at the onset of her presence. it always sounds like someone is knocking and i answer for her every time. she is a layered woman. an ocean. the orishas commune at her shores. everyone thinks that she is some kind of miracle because she has learned that water is the portal. i know it is because she is a god.

when was the first time you realized you were a god?

what season was it?

did you smile and slither into yourself while welcoming yourself home?

did your heart grow heavy at the thought of all the people and places you had to shed?

did you finally become both naked and vulnerable in the right hands?

did you learn the difference?

-lessons

you are an experience disguised as a woman.

i've seen the way you water yourself.

you come undone and bloom ferociously.

your lovers treat you like something that should be plucked
and possessed but you are the type of woman that requires
freedom to grow where you please.

write me down.

read me.

bookmark your favorite parts.

-i like the way your hands cradle my spine

i'm always letting the people i love in.

i'm always unfolding daring you to go deeper.

only those familiar with the divine can see what isn't seen with

the naked eye.

i should tell you i see you.

you are made up of waves and honey.

energy, thick and intense, cascading and crashing againstme.

this energy sits between us magical and stirring.

it keeps me close to you.

i know you feel me.

show me where you hide your softness. i will keep it safe.

-vulnerability

some days magic is you sitting in the silence with me, books in hand while your head is on my chest and you can't tell which limbs belong to whom. other days magic is your mouth swallowing the ocean you created between my thighs.

there are some things i can show you better than i can tell you.

my hands know all the places that turn you into a wildfire and a poem.

my tongue writing a secret code only visible in certain light.

in certain love.

come. let me remind you that god exists everywhere.

-reminders

you have mastered the art of touching my mind before you touch my body.

i have a thing for hands.

i have a thing for women who are good with their hands.

women who can build things
women who can heal things

with their hands.

i keep imagining what my body would feel like underneath your

hands.

would you knead my flesh like clay?

would you caress me like brush strokes against canvas?

what kind of god would you make of me?

-touch

after you shove words down my throat and kiss poems up the back of my knees my arms beg to embrace you. i love when you lay your head on my chest. you match the smile that has drawn itself across my face. i kiss your forehead. you kiss my collarbone. some of our most intimate conversations have taken place between these walls and i am convinced that the closet thing to heaven is us in this bed.

-pillow talk

i love you. i want to show you what it is like to not be alone in

this world.

i cannot tell you how much i love the smell of fresh white

sheets and you. this bed feels so empty when you are not in it

with me. i love lazy mornings with you. naked. falling in and

out of sleep. fucking. smoking blunts. whiskey or wine for

breakfast followed by you, again and again and again.

you move me. you know how to pull love right out of me. i

surrender effortlessly for you. i could not stop pouring into you

even if i tried.

every poem is a confession of my love for you.

treat them like your favorite vinyl.

spend hours combing through my collection.

do you remember the first time i saw you?

divine and dressed in the love you have for me.

you make forever feel possible.

i knew that you deserved to know what

worship means outside

of the church.

you are heaven on earth and i'd like to enter you.

you spent last night putting your life back together and turning

me into a poem. i want you to know that i will still be here in

the morning.

-the morning after

i should tell you I keep you safe in the center of my heart. i'm

always staring at you trying to feel you out while my mind is

swallowing the art that is you. from the moment we met i've

been studying you. i take pleasure in l(earning) you. there is

something inviting about the softness you hide. i see you. the

divine in you. you keep me at a safe distance, but if you knew

me you'd know that i've never liked safe. you're afraid

someone will break something in you that is already so fragile.

something that you're still putting back together. you would like

me to run away from you, but a woman such as myself doesn't

run from the light. i run towards it.

-intimacy is a spiritual practice

if i had the time

i would've traveled the length of your body this morning

exploring the terrain that is your flesh trying to see how many

times i can make you call out to your god before work.

-morning sex

one day i am going to marry you. i'm going to spend the rest of

my life kissing your wounds, being your biggest fan and

celebrating your victories. even the small ones.

you will fuck me in our brooklyn brownstone on lazy mornings

when the sun is peeking up from the horizon

morning is just about to come

we will come together.

with the crescendo of day

and we will gather our mess of love right before our children

enter the room and i will wonder if they can hear the butterflies

in my stomach for you or if they can see how my heart still

swoons.

-marriage

25

i felt magic and saw a miracle at two:thirty in the afternoon.

that is how i knew you were supposed to be here. you

opened me up and you have not stopped pouring into me and

i'm still not quite sure what to do with myself. you commanded

the attention of every cell in my body that i didn't even realize

until i was standing naked baring all of my wounds in front of

you that my spirit had undressed itself for you.

one day we are going to own a home near the ocean. when the

weather is just right we will come outside and sit as the waves

beat against the shore. we will engage in conversation and

mid-sentence i'll realize how much i rise in love with you

every day. i will always be the right amount of soft for you. we'll

laugh, drink wine, listen to some music and slow dance in our

own little paradise. some days we'll call our friends to join us.

you'll keep them company while i cook. you'll come hug me

playfully from behind, slightly pouting, because you're ready to

eat and for me to join you. dinner is ready. we all sit to eat.

i reach over to rub your thigh and then i take your hand in

mine. i'll look around the table at all the beautiful women and

men including you and the light that pours from them filling the

room. i am full of gratitude and silently thanking the universe

for a wonderful life of magic and love.

-manifestation no. 1

you are the kind of happiness not many people find in this lifetime.

i am not afraid of your dark.

the corners of you that you have yet to face.

the battles across your heart that you are still fighting.

i will learn to exist in the night and sit under your moon.

my heart full

resembling you.

                              -for the women who run with the wolves

it is saturday morning and i've just woken up from my slumber because my arms did not feel you. half groggy. half wondering where you are. you're on the stoop with a piping hot cup of jasmine green tea and your journal. the weather is inviting and you wanted to enjoy mother nature's splendor before you started your day. i find you and sit next to you. you share your tea with me. we don't say much. this love has always been enough even in the silence. i grab your hand and hold it in mine. the butterflies in my stomach start to flutter again. it is because i know your secret. you get up to pray and manifest things on the pages of your journal. i must tell you that there is nothing more beautiful than a woman who has something to believe in.

everything that happens to you each year makes you even

more desirable. wisdom looks so good on you.

thank you for leaving me.

can i have you?

you already do.

i've been waiting here all day for you to call and say you'll

meet me so i can give you my heart.

there she was with the anticipation of my arrival dripping from

her brow. she was never a patient woman, but she always

waited for what she wanted. i watched her from across the

room before i made my way to her. she was slim thick and it

was the way her collarbones protruded that made you want

to leave trails of kisses on them. she wore mystery like a cloak

guarding all of her secrets. she wore her black proudly. she

was a sea of curves beckoning anyone with enough courage to

swim in her depth and here i was equally unafraid of her calm

and the turbulence that existed inside of her.

-i will never tremble at the thought of loving you

there are days that I do not want quiet.

i want your moans to be guttural as my name

barely slips out past the breaths you are trying to catch.

.

her body a constellation of stars

her milky way

flowing like honey between celestial thighs

i want to spend the rest of my life in love and laughing with you.

i am enamored by the way you bloom.

by the way each layer of you unfolds.

-black velvet petunia

you remind me of a garden.

melanin rich like the soil.

i want to bury my hands in you.

and feel the coolness of the earth.

i want to plant something here inside you.

i'll start with love.

i am drawn to you because our inner children play well together.

-twin flame

i am a sure woman.

it never takes me long to make up my mind about you.

you are a familiar feeling.

a fire always smoldering in me.

from the back of the café i enjoy one of my favorite things, people watching. humans are capricious slippery amusing endearing beings. i find pleasure in the facial expressions, hurried aesthetic movements and the vulnerabilities that seep through the cracks when people are just being themselves. i pull out my notepad + begin to scribble down my thoughts. suddenly. i'm pulled from my thoughts by a woman who walked by smelling so delicious. curves intact, her natural hair playfully all over her head in a fro. i study her intensely. i notice how her lips curl before her face breaks into a smile. raw umber is the exact color brown of her eyes. i notice how her collarbones speak of summer mornings in the city when she laughs & tilts her head back. the woman carries herself like a god. i can tell she is a composed ocean of waves that could become turbulent if you test her. something about her energy filled up an entire room without apology. the woman began to make her way towards my table. the butterflies in my stomach start to flutter and i wonder if this god of a woman can hear them coming alive for her. she said you've been observing me from the moment i walked in the door. i smile + say well it looks like you've been observing me as well. we introduce ourselves to one another. she says most people shrink when i come into a room, but you, you expanded. i say oceans do not shrink, we expand. i'd like to get to know you. may i have your number? the woman laughs. before she could say anything else i say you seem like the type of woman who needs to be in control and i'm not intimidated by that. here is my number and a few things you should know about me. i am part hopeful romantic, part savage, free spirited, writer, lover of women and my god is a black woman with curves. i hope you find me worthy of your time. i'd like to spend a day immortalizing you. the woman looks at her watch. intrigued she says and how do you intend on doing that? i smile. by turning you into this poem.

-come. let me make a poem out of you

i am here to remind you that i am deep and stable enough to

withstand any of your storms. i am your anchor. this kind of

love can never be destroyed. only transformed.

-alchemy

the arch of your back reminds me of a crescent moon.

i'll come home after a long day. you'll hug me + let me linger inside your arms for a while. with my head nestled underneath your chin i inhale you. you always smell so good. you'll say get dressed we're going out. i oblige without a fuss. we'll end up in a dimly lit lounge with a good music selection. i"ll slide in the booth next to you. my mouth waters at the way your thighs spread like butter. we order food + drinks. between conversing, laughing + flirting i will have forgotten what had me upset earlier. i stare at you in amazement as you speak. i love you pours from my mouth. silence. your eyes soften. you smile and ask why? i never break eye contact. i love you because you mean what you say and say what you mean. you don't half ass anything. i love you because one of your superpowers is being able to make time stop. you command my attention, so much so, that everything around us blurs into the background. you always make me feel like we are the only ones in the room. you pour peace back into me effortlessly. you lean into me. my hand finds your thigh. biting your bottom lip you say i love you too and tonight i'm going to show you what other kind of magic i can do. home. you lead me to the bedroom. body + thighs already begging to feel the weight of you. you gently fold me into origami. orgasm after orgasm. you make art out of me.

-moana lisa

keep loving me like you're seeing god for the first time.

you'll come home + unravel on our kitchen floor after suffering an unexpected disappointment or loss. i'll remind you that it's okay to take the weight of the world off your shoulders. i"ll take the thread of you lying on the floor + scoop it up in my hands. i'll whisper come here. you'll come without a fuss and press your body against me as your tears stain my shirt. i hold you for what feels like an eternity. we go to the bedroom. you rest and i take care of you for the evening. i can still see small parts of you trying to hold it together. i'll say it's okay, come undone at the seams. spill everywhere. tomorrow i'll pour back into you what the world drained from you.

-restoration

you deserve to be fucked well, mentally.

does the stroke of her pen move you like mine?

does she hit every spot?

does her pen know the places in you that ache for words to fill them?

is her ink thicker than mine?

does she form oceans inside of you?

oceans that make a mess between your thighs?

inhale

me.

i won't

let

you

come

down

off

this

high.

you are a work of art.

your brown flesh housing all of the masterpieces that

encompass you.

i stand and stare.

every layer of you leaves me breathless.

my favorite piece is your heart.

still good in this cruel world.

still gold.

-(muse)um

you are a sea of curves and i want to swim in you.

i'd like to know how the weight of my body feels against yours.

i'd like to become familiar with the sound of your soft raspy

moans that escape your mouth when i first enter you.

-depth

remove your shoes and fears before you enter my home.

from the moment i connected with you i have been studying you.

your eyes tell me everything i need to know.

your smile could bring anyone to their knees.

your thighs keep hesitation clenched between them.

while your mind begs to be stimulated.

come. sit with me.

can i offer you a drink or would you like me to pour into you?

you should know i am an ocean.
vast. unyielding. insatiable.

there is no time to be afraid. only time to do what we feel.

will you trust me?

or do you wear life jackets in all of your relation ships?

you ever met a woman that shifts you just by existing?

i care about you. can i take care of you? every time you deny

me such pleasure my heart breaks a little. i want to show you

that you deserve the peace and love you give.

-spoiling you is a love language

i want to leave my poem in the corner of your mouth.

-slow kissing

one day you're going to walk through the door after a long day of work. i won't hear your footsteps over marvin gaye singing in the background. you'll stop and lean against the wall on the entry way just before you enter the kitchen. a smile will draw itself across your face as you watch me in my boy shorts and t-shirt dancing, singing, and being silly in the kitchen. you'll find your way behind me. you'll press yourself against me as you place a kiss on the space between my earlobe and neck. we melt at the same time. i'll pour you a glass of your favorite wine and by the time we kiss, hug, and laugh you'll have already forgotten that you've had a bad day.

-sometimes home is a person

i have reserved a place for you in me.

one that will always open at the onset of your presence.

how could i ever forget what you make me feel?

you. dressed in divinity and drenched in saltwater.

you stood in the center of me and was never afraid to keep

exploring me no matter how far it took you away from the

shore because you knew i would always be home.

   -for women whose curiosity and love outweigh their fear

my love looks good on you. you wear freedom well.

i want to write poems in the tone of your lover's voice.

the kind that make you wet.

the kind that make you surrender to yourself.

the kind that will not allow you to take your eyes off the pages

because you like words being shoved down your throat.

they will look at you and think that you are hard.

they will see scars and think that you are a mountain too high

to climb.

they will think that your wounds are valleys that are too deep.

they will see me and wonder how i survived you.

i will tell them that you are not a woman i had to survive.

you are a woman who needed to know that she wasn't alone.

i saw you beyond your scars and the wounds you are still

nursing.

i saw your light illuminating all of the places in you that need

healing.

you are too divine to pour into those who do not see you.

-godly women

you make me laugh

the kind of laughs

that make me feel

like we are the only ones

in the room.

you are both a seductress and a healer.

i want to know what it feels like to be loved by you. i want to know how your love would transform me.

you are a walking contradiction.

a simple complexitiy.

every conversation reveals another layer of you.

like a bonus track on a favorite album.

you are intoxicating.

i can never get enough of you.

there is never enough time to savor you.

to fall into the spaces of you.

i am coming undone

but i am not unraveling

she is holding me together

with her eyes.

                                        with her love.

my hands do no justice to the magic that is your tongue.

i woke up craving the sound of you.

call me at two a.m. to tell me you can't sleep because a poem
is being birth inside of you.

i love you.

i want you.

on purpose.

there is comfort in knowing someone like you exists.

i want to travel the world and share my sunday's and summers with you.

i have carried your prayers

licked.

bitten.

kissed.

written.

scratched.

across my flesh

to the gods in our dreams.

don't ever stop feeling me.

when was the last time you took the weight of the world off

your shoulders? when was the last time you got undressed

and you took off your fears? when was the last time intimacy

knocked and you answered? love has been trying to get close

to you. when was the last time someone showed a genuine

interest in learning you and you wholeheartedly let them in?

not everyone is out to harm you. when was the last time you

explored yourself and found god? what did you say to yourself

when you realized that who you've been looking for is you?

what did it feel like when you saw everything you need already

inside of you? your energy is holy. you are powerful enough

to heal yourself. they call women like you witches. you are a

tangible miracle. you are faith personified. how can you believe

in everyone else, but yourself?

over tea.

over coffee.

tell me all of your dreams.

we can spend an entire day constructing their wings.

you speak the language of my ancestors to me.

you are everything i want in a woman.

you are art. poetry. music. free.

i have waited lifetimes for you.

let me be clear

i am aiming my pen at your heart.

-certainty

i.   energy cannot be created or destroyed
            nothing ends
            every atom remembers your name

ii.   your name exploding in my mouth
            staining my insides
            leaving flowers in my heart

iii.   as i spoke
            my words kept
            reaching for god.
            for you.

iv.   the moon
            scintillating
            imitates your light

v.   i'm drawn to you
            like a moth
            to a flame

-for sonia

you touch me like i am everything you asked god for.

underneath your hands i become poetry.

this is the alchemy that you do.

www.ingramcontent.com/pod-product-compliance
Lightning Source LLC
Chambersburg PA
CBHW050948030426
42339CB00007B/341